LOEW'S
TRIBORO

LOEW'S TRIBORO

POEMS BY
JOHN ALLMAN

March 12, 2004
Katonah

*This is for Jennifer and Minas,
our wonderful neighbors!*

*Much Love,
Le Père*

A NEW DIRECTIONS BOOK

Some of the poems in this book have been published in *Blackbird: A Journal of Literature and the Arts* ("The Kidnapping," "Lung"), *Crazyhorse* ("The Asphalt Jungle I and II," published as a single poem), *5 AM* ("Dropout," "Eleanor," "Glare"), *Full Circle: A Journal of Poetry and Prose* ("So," "The Ride Home"), *Kestrel* ("Cutting His Wrist"), *The Michigan Quarterly Review* ("Payoff"), *North Dakota Quarterly* ("Taking the Case," "The Stairs"), *Slope* ("The Cad," "The Picture"), *The Yale Review* ("Love").

Frontispiece, courtesy of the Theatre Historical Society of America, Elmhurst, Illinois

Book design by Sylvia Frezzolini Severance
Manufactured in the United States of America
New Directions Books are printed on acid-free paper.
First published as New Directions Paperbook 989 in 2004
Published simultaneously in Canada by Penguin Books Canada Ltd.

Library of Congress Cataloging-in-Publication Data

Allman, John, 1935–
Loew's triboro : poems / by John Allman.
    p. cm.
"A new directions book."
ISBN 0-8112-1577-6
1. Astoria (New York, N.Y.)—Poetry. 2. Motion picture theaters—Poetry. 3. Motion pictures—Poetry. I. Title.
PS3551.L46L64 2004
811'.54—dc22
                            2003025680

New Directions Books are published for James Laughlin
by New Directions Publishing Corporation,
80 Eighth Avenue, New York, NY 10011

For my parents,
John King Allman (1912–58)
and Helen Burghard Allman (1912–80)

CONTENTS

LOEW'S TRIBORO

It was easy as lying to our mothers. As living in Queens
        across from Manhattan, walking over
the bridge connecting three boroughs, looking
down on the nut house on Ward's Island, one of us
        dribbling a basketball. Eggs in our

pockets, we sneaked into the Loew's theater through
        the back door. The old vaudeville stage
behind the movie screen moving with the shadow of
Bogart and his lisp. One of us just out of jail for sticking
        up a drugstore. His father leaving him

there two extra days to teach him a lesson. We climbed
        up the ladder along the side of the
screen, behind a fake Renaissance curtain, looked out at
the audience in the dark, the glowing cigarettes, Hank,
        whose father ran a dry-goods store

on Steinway Street, slipping his hand under a girl's skirt.
        Checking the material. A script
flickering at our loins. The newsreel releasing survivors
into sunlight, arms thin as the stripes on their pajamas.
        Eleanor's father on the corner of Broadway

waving pamphlets for the Labor Party. Eleanor not yet
        in her marine boyfriend's room getting
shot to death. We reached the little balcony, the Wurlitzer
organ draped with an old carpet, the bad smell of Father
        Flaherty's breath. We kept going.

At the top of the screen, from behind a decorative
        molding, we saw our neighbors sucking
Black Crows, rolling darkness in their mouths. And
we started. The eggs cool from Sonny's aunt's
        refrigerator flew across

the night sky blinking down from light-bulb space. They
        landed like doves breaking apart on Hank's
chest, a gooey wound on the girl's skirt. They slid out of our
hands like ghosts, uncle's loud jokes descending at his
        sister's second wedding, groans

splurting in the night, a rifled mischief rotating in the air,
        concussed, spun by history's grooves,
while Jerry down there with his polio leg in a brace
raised himself on the splattered yolky arms of his seat
        and roared, shaking his fist.

LOVE

SO

It wasn't just the war. Or wearing a little officer's uniform,
    the leather strap across my chest
like a seat belt so I wouldn't hit my head on the future.
My sister turning so red from measles she lit up the dingy
    back room where mother siphoned

electricity from the hall fixture. It wasn't poverty that pulled
    darkness down. Maybe the slap
across the face, my mother's glasses flying across the kitchen,
my father swaying like a branch some bird just left, flying away
    from emptiness. But two nights

later, I'd hear them grunting in the bedroom, so it wasn't homily
    or forgiveness. That's not why
my eyes dilated against the light, against the laws of the body and
reason. Or why they opened wide in the cigarette smoke of movie
    balconies. Seeing what wasn't there.

LOVE

The novel lying on the table, its front cover up, no likeness of any-one on it, no landscape on the dust jacket, the film already running, she knows she is trying the story for a second time. Trying to get it right. Being a leggy blonde in shorts and silk blouse with shoulder pads, a stylish turban wound around her head. Aware he's the hired man. The one who picked up the help-wanted sign blown down in a rainstorm, the other sign still up there banging in the wind, promis-ing lunch and dinner. Her husband's roadside restaurant where she works. Her husband's promise. What hungry men think they want.

Now she's swimming with him near the cliffs in high tide on a moon-lit evening. They come out of the water and she laughs in his arms, the two of them clasping each other. He tells her how much he wants her, how he's wandered through small towns ever since the war ended, looking for her, when the motorcycle policeman in jodhpurs was squinting at him, and the district attorney, a fedora knocked back on his head, drove up in a coupe and gave a lift to the smart-ass veteran in rolled-up sleeves. Who was him. Which is how he got here.

And he looked up at the sign. The husband clapped him on the back. She came out needing a light, looking him up and down, disgusted. Which says how much she likes him. And she knows later the hus-band is drinking too much, doing his accounts. He hardly looks at her because she's like dinnerware that hasn't broken yet. Debts float-ing a slow blackjack overhead. And that's how it happens. The sec-ond chance. With him. The hired man.

The question being how long she believes in accidents. The wet road, the drinking, him unshaven, hearing police sirens that aren't there, her hand under his shirt—which is a lot of skin just after the war— the California coastline a kind of lumpy snake that bumps them off the road. And he's crushed by the steering wheel. She's leaning back from the dash, blood all over her slacks. And he's in front of his restaurant, on a ladder, putting up another sign. The husband.

After *The Postman Always Rings Twice* (1946)

ELEANOR

She lit a cigarette up there in the balcony, her lipstick
       imprinting the smoke before it even
reached her lungs, her hand itching for a reason, an automatic,
something she could snap a clip into. Boys showing up,
       one by one sitting next to her, slipping

a hand under her sweater, while she rubbed the bulges in their
       pants and puffed smoke into the shaft
of light from the projector, laughing when they sidled out of the
aisle in their sticky underwear. There wasn't anyone didn't know
       her name in the halls of the high school.

Or in the front seat of cars where they dreamt of the blow jobs
       they'd never get and waited for her to walk
home from her job in the dry-goods store. Maybe it was her father's
Labor Party pamphlets, the beating he took on Broadway, next to
       Woolworth's, or the way she breathed so

heavily through a deviated septum, as if she always had a cold. Or
       blame her sister's weight. Mother's long blood-
hound face. Maybe it was the way a woman walked on screen, how
she leaned against a wall, waiting for a light, every guy in a dark suit
       coming up to her with his hand cupping fire.

THE SCRIPT

Another time banging on the door like the iceman, years
     dripping from his shoulders.
What should I say in my fedora, what should my sister do,
rising from her couch all doped up? Mother nervously sipping
     tea, in this movie we're suddenly

written into, the door shuddering to his blows, my father
     locked out again.
One morning I slouch into the street, sneering at myself
in the grocery window, smoking Raleighs, stealing *The Mirror*
     from a newsstand, to see what

war is on. What's at the RKO. Dreaming, my sister pushes some
     old guy out the window
of his office, because he can't keep his hands to himself. He's the
therapist she sleeps with, see, the one who tells her how sick she
     really is. The next night,

after a few drinks, a lot of disgust, she dreams she jumps out the
     window. There's hell to pay
because our mother is afraid to wake her when she's screaming.
How many people can you look after? Me, I'm just the moody
     detective looking at my sister's photo.

THE STAIRS

She used to crawl up to her passed-out father's room on hands and knees, mother the boss's daughter who married beneath contempt, stretched out like the white-ruffed blanket the daughter still wraps around her legs. Then they were gone, like the canary, like the kitten. Just gone. The stairs twisting upwards into a Möbius strip reversing whatever she did. Like her first boyfriend, the penniless kid with all that spunk, who left on the freight without her, what's he doing here now, back from the war, wearing extravagant neckties, on his arm a blonde with accommodating lisp?

There are just too many women with frightened eyes. But business is good. The factory spreading from the river to weed-grown fields. She's got her dimple-chin husband now the D. A. and it rains when she sends a lover off. Whatever she makes in her factory, it isn't toasters or vacuum tubes but a kind of sorrow that tastes like metal. Like girlhood. The memory of pushing her aunt down the stairs—that woman's hair pulled back, tied into a bun, parsimonious lips, the bound breasts, her stiff-snake walking stick a teacher's pointer tapping the wrong answer. Who isn't born to die? Mother's canary on its back, claws curled around nothing. The kitten caught on the stairs, the stick in the aunt's hand whistling through the air, freight cars rumbling through the factory yard. Her own breasts budding, rain blowing against the window, the tutor's son licking at her ear. The aunt crumpled on the landing below.

Years pass. Cars grow sleek. The old boyfriend stuck here all of a sudden in the town he didn't even know he was passing through. "It's not anyone's fault. It's what people want. And how hard it is to get it." The blonde with him like a flash of light from a dead star, carrying herself forward from a bad beginning, used to being burned, always hanging on, given one-to-five for wearing another woman's fur she didn't know wasn't hers for smiling and spreading, her time between men less than the life of mayflies. "Okay, sister, you did a swell job. Now blow." And the man would never know doubt. Never look back. Never hear the pouring out of herself like salt.

But the other one. The niece on the stairs, the owner, the wife in a beaded hood. Great shoes, great legs. Let it all burn. Let it scald the mind. She's put away a gym instructor. A fullback. An engineer. A mechanic. "This all began a long time ago." In her dream, there's a knife sticking in her back. The rain begins again. Wind whips dark sulfurous smoke away from her chimneys, the blast furnaces, cooling profits. The metal sign on her building clanging against the eaves. Her trucks hooded with canvas.

If she shoved her aunt, there must be cruelty to deal with awareness. If she's a bird inside a cage, it is not sickness trying to get out. If she owns the hotel, the factory, the garage, there is prosperity in war and failure. If she needs room to breathe, there must be others with no right to live. If she handles her husband's automatic, there is softness to receive the hard. If the boy she once loved has returned a man, there is thunder without rain. If she feels like a real woman, she's been there before. If she cries, there is greed in someone's practiced heart. If she strips away her name, she will forget the sound of a cane whacking on the stairs.

After *The Strange Love of Martha Ivers* (1946)

THE CAD

TREATS

Mama's old boyfriend is on the front page of *The Daily News,*
      his mouth a black hole, legs spread out like a
dancer fallen on his back. The cop a buttoned-up elf pointing
to the dark alley the guy had run out of like a prince gone bad
      in some ballet. "He had a sweet smile," she says.

Imagine Mama in a movie called *Escape,* sitting in the front
      seat of a Model A, loading cartridges into
a .38, her lover in the white Stetson grinning. The owner
of the General Store they're parked in front of is hoping
      to close early, thinking of sweeping out

the church, the Kansas sun sinking like a broken pendulum.
      They go in, her purse heavy as a womb
hanging wrong, and she says, "I feel like something sweet!" Later,
two gunshots, the Ford bouncing down the dirt road, caramel and
      bits of nut stuck in their teeth.

Maybe some B-movie guy left his seed in her. Maybe you were
      a bad birth. That's why your father comes home
late, red-eyed, stinking, grief-stricken. He can't remember any
loving. "Are you sure he's mine?" He play-boxes you against
      the wall in the kitchen, the smell of cold

pot roast and potatoes like something rising into the air in church
      at mass, the gong sounding
so you don't look at it, so you don't see the face of God suddenly
visible, cheap as bread. "You bastard," she says. Today, she's
      pushing a baby carriage, varicose veins

running up her legs like rivers you memorize for a test. She
　　　breast-feeds your brother right there
in front of you in the ice-cream parlor booth and nobody knows
you snatched two Baby Ruths on the way in. That it's only right
　　　you take what's yours. What you deserve.

FEDORA

In 1882 Sarah Bernhardt wore a felt hat in Victorien
Sardou's play about the woman, Fédora, who fell in love
with the killer of her fiancé.

Soft as the shadow it makes over the eyes, smooth
       between the fingers, take your father's
Royal Deluxe, the creased shape of its crown, the odor
of hair oil. Darkness cast by a snapped-down brim
       makes a thin face

sneer. Four fingers of the right hand sliding into the pocket
       of a sharkskin suit, your thumb
exposed like a nerve, like a foreign word in a sentence,
your voice ambiguous, cigarette smoke curling into your
       eyes. You talk like someone who

broke out of Sing Sing, spotlights flashing from the towers.
       Someone outside,
waiting in a Packard. All the screws yelling your name.
Think of a kiss in the front seat of the old Dodge under
       the broken street light.

Boys roaming the streets, the soft fuzz on their cheeks,
       their oatmeal single-breasted
tweeds begging for a Whippet or Premier, walnut brown,
willow green, a Stratoliner adding a little height,
       deepening their voices.

HOOKY

We got out of there, we made off. The forged notes from
      our mothers held up to the light by the Dean
of Boys, our grandmothers' recycled deaths, while we
rocked on the "G" train to Queensboro Plaza, to Times
      Square, Hubert's Flea Circus,

the hermaphrodite Albert and Alberta gyrating in a porthole
      window, showing his womanly breast.
We ate overcooked spaghetti in Romeo's, crawled out
the bathroom window to avoid paying, boasting about
      our fathers in their leaky

'38 Chevies and Dodges with tar roofs, the girlfriends
      we didn't have. Pity wasted. Save it
for the really fucked up! The truant officer waving his
three-fingered hand in our faces, before he got canned
      for being a Communist.

Before his kids got beat up. We were free as cowboys
      heating beans in a pan, coughing up
cigarettes, peeling coupons from Raleighs to redeem
the gift of our lungs. The girls in their gym suits playing
      field hockey behind the school,

all that promise, all those green bloomers, while we sneaked
      into the Ladies Room in the Triboro theater,
past the anteroom with gilded chairs, looking in empty stalls
for a pubic hair, a Kotex napkin, anything that was the touch
      of woman.

DROPOUT

Mrs. Fox the Trig teacher said no one had ever cut her
        classes the way he did. He pulled a 16
on the Regents. The truant officer, his index and ring
fingers stumpy from the war or maybe from the radiator
        fan of an old Chevy,

kept prodding him in the chest as if he'd fallen asleep
        at his post. They called his father
at work, and his father caught him in the street, said
he'd take a bat to him. They put him in a special class
        of bright kids and told them

never to speak to him. So he stole homework. Stole
        hubcaps. Shoplifted in Strauss Auto Parts.
Sold everything to the gas station where he worked
weekends. Drank Seagram's 7 in the Loew's balcony,
        watching gunfighters twitch a smile.

Stuck a pin through the telephone wire in the phone
        booth to make short-circuit calls to his girl-
friend, who kept telling him he could finish school. Whose
mother wanted her to hang up. At night sometimes the
        planes from La Guardia flew so low it was

like thunder in the alleyway, like bombardment, the whizz
        of mortar shells, sky collapsing
on his uncovered head where he slept on a ragged couch.
The iceman in the morning clinking outside like a corporal
        collecting dog tags from the dead.

THE CAD

Cigarette, always the cigarette, held between thumb and forefinger, brought to his lips like a gibe. Her hand half covering her mouth, the white evening gown sagging off a shoulder. She can't pay her gambling debts, her husband unable to leave his wheelchair, to stand the shock of what she is. But this man knows about the bonds, that she can get in the safe in the paneled study with the classic nudes, if she has the nerve. Which is why he looks out the casino windows at the lake and talks of Tangiers, the foreign agents who pay. How did she think her husband made his money before all those workers died in the mine? The government closing its eyes. "Surely you know about the canary." Falling from its perch. He says, "*Gaz.*" Lights another cigarette, in a long holder, its tip clenched between his teeth. "One must live to sing another day." He pats her hand.

After the war, the violet-eyed girl he thought he cared for, even when her father lost everything in Poland and she loved some ministry assistant with his hair slicked back, a smile empty as a sugar sack. That man unfortunately caught with military plans and some trollop at the hotel. Some actress. Who just happens to know the drama critic of *The Times*. You know who. With the acid pen. But the girlfriend, the little fool, flings herself off a bridge. What is one to do? The heart a candy thing. Always dissolving.

He pats his mouth dry, looks out across the Loire, this trip he's taking, composing his final letter to friends. But not quite. An American woman in long skirt and a sweater. Conical breasts.

Ridiculous. Delicious. Her first time abroad. His breath heavy with the flavor of Turkish cigarettes, hers sweet with Ohio dew. "Good morning!" Her thighs the creamy undulations of small-town tides, her movements beneath him carrying him out to sea. That's how it could be. If he weren't so bored.

For George Sanders (1906–72)

THE APRON

THE APRON

Her mother's last illness tied behind her back: knotted peonies and buttercups spill across her abdomen. Faded petals hem her knees, birds fluttering around them like the pigeons outside her window on the job where she worked typing and filing, before she quit, before she stayed home with mother. She's always here in the same apartment, with the little man at the front desk in the lobby buzzing people in; that sound different from the soft chime of the bell outside her door; her sister in a downtown store selling sweaters, lingerie, waiting to be seen: long legs, blonde hair. Scorn. What ambition needs. What the little man in the lobby is always staring at. This one at home has to be here to let people in, though no one arrives, except her sister, changing clothes, rushing away. Nothing on the stove. No grease crackling in a pan.

The sister in the apron leans back in mother's chair and imagines the boyfriend. Not the one who writes for the papers, not the has-been actor looking in a shop window at mannequins, the sister in there tacking up a price, $9.99, twitching her heart-shaped bum. (This one, in the apartment, looks great in the one-piece black bathing suit later at the pool—after the news, the killing, the ID at the morgue—good enough to be taped inside a soldier's helmet, looking for something to be stuck onto, in a boyfriend's arms, up against his chest, inhaling the odor trapped beneath his shirt, if she only knew where he was. Who he was.)

There's a sound she's hearing, a sound getting through. She gets up from the meadow in her lap, answering the door for the detective who's been waved through the lobby, who's been fingering the chimes like birdsong since the day began, who right away notices her face is like her sister's only a little chubby. He looks down at the washed-out blue bells circling her covered navel. He almost weeps to tell her that her sister's dead. The beautiful one. He's choking up, in the apartment with end tables and a soiled antimacassar where the dead sister used to lay back her head. He would have pulled off her shoes and massaged her aching feet, if she'd have let him—if she hadn't despised him staring at her through the window day after day, when his shift was over, when the oily sweat of petty thieves still clung to his nostrils, his hands, and he held a handkerchief to his face and breathed her in. And looked. How he looked.

He hasn't yet seen little sister at the hotel pool, legs good enough to be photographed. But she doesn't swim too well and there's nothing to notice in the water except her feet thrashing. She climbs out dripping, and showers, and dries off. She walks out into the street, the apron on under her black coat. He's following her, trying to figure out where she was the night the other one was strangled. And who was in the closet of the hotel room where it happened—and smoking, because he found the butts. Which is why he breathes with difficulty, knowing how it was in the last minutes, someone peering from the closet, while her dress came off, hips filling out the black slip before it fell to the floor. Him not there to stop what happened next.

Maybe she had to die. Giving everyone ideas, a kind of future, the other sales girls, the short-order cook in the coffee shop, cheap houses going up on Long Island, veterans opening little gas stations as they said they would when buddies were dying in their arms on Omaha Beach or Iwo Jima or in Bastogne. Changing the order of things. The enemy now someone in the closet, opening the warped wooden doors a crack. Wanting a cigarette real bad. The detective in despair later tacking up her picture in his room. Votive candles burning all around her. He can't stop what he keeps seeing: her in the smoky light, calling for help, calling his name. And he wasn't there.

She's back home, the sister in the apron, walking past the little man seated at the front desk in the lobby of her apartment house, the little man with sad eyes looking up at her (like a man shining his flash on a picture in his foxhole, the enemy somewhere else) looking right through her unbuttoned coat, at the apron, imagining her beautiful legs, his nicotine fingers the color of worn shoes, while she stops to chat, enjoying his gaze. As if she lay there among the embroidered forget-me-nots, the bushy dahlias, the green edging neat as cut grass. A small translucent circle made by butter, a tiny window he sees through, what he couldn't see before: she's in the kitchen, apron taut. A pot boiling over. Someone blowing cigarette smoke that swirls over the stove and drifts out toward the living room, the armchair—the open newspaper with tomorrow's story about the murdered clerk who worked the lobby of this building.

After *I Wake Up Screaming* (1941)

TAKING THE CASE

THE KIDNAPPING

Grandmother left her youngest child, Alice, with a neighbor
      on the top floor because she was moving
into another building where she could be the super. She didn't
want the baby in the middle of all that mess. Her husband, Blackie,
      driving up and down Tenth Avenue,

delivering electrical supplies—plugs, cords, little relay boxes like
      the black recorders plucked years later
from drowned airliners, a voice behind Blackie already saying,
"We're going down, we're going down!" The neighbor disappeared
      with Alice. No note, no nothing. Just

the empty apartment. Blackie had a few more drinks near the docks
      on Twelfth Avenue, near the German
freighters, talking about the Lindbergh baby. Burly men grew misty-
eyed and cursed Bruno Hauptmann. The newsreel ran on and on.
      After mother grew up and married the ex-

bootleg driver with the melancholy face, maybe she thought her
      sister could be recovered
if she named her own daughter Alice. The baby growing into a
pigtailed girl inside my sister, who woke nights afraid she couldn't
      breathe, who sleepwalked

toward the kitchen window with the loose pane that popped out
      the next morning and floated down
into the alley like a transparent soul the neighbors looked through
before it crashed near the super sweeping up clothespins and bottle
      caps. Whose hand was it in art class drew

the little house with the smoking chimney and three children
instead of two, arms and legs spread
out, spinning in the air? Who first bled through bargain cotton
panties? My sister clawing at her face, something pinching her
abdomen, twisting up an eye.

TAKING THE CASE

It's what the blonde wants him to believe about her story. It's what the dick wanted him to remember about his past. It's why he walks through rusted shadows of the El that cut across three city streets and he hears confessions from all sides. They want him to explain who they are, their voices hovering like the notes of a string quartet, that buzz in the air the hesitation of melody. What's childhood but a father who can't give up his women, a mother not allowed to take her son away from the hot, noisy *calle*. The dark young girl with the velvet skin said she would love him under the faithful stars forever and then she said good-by. The body a bag of lies. Take the stairs, how an aunt tumbles down the spiral into a heap. He was already on Riverside Drive under the streetlamp, lighting up, thinking about the cigarette case found in a vestibule. The wife *in flagrante*. The big smile of the blue-collar boyfriend who didn't speak French, couldn't understand her uptown friends or her evenings of perfect silence at the Hotel Colón, the Pension Isabella. Her suitcase with decals like scabs. Her gun at her throat when he leaves. Accident or intent, the same slashing odor, the blood-mapped wall. Take justice out of the thing, out of accident, out of unconscious spite—get rid of the unconscious—it's what the old stripper lies about, hiding her bottle, waving off men who left before her looks crashed: "I want nothing but air on all sides of me." It's why his father left his mother. The stars twittering like traffic lights up and down the avenue, where everything falls to earth.

After the life and work of Cornell Woolrich (1903–68)

MRS. WHITE

The first dead person he'd ever seen. Laid out in her
      living room,
the sound of traffic outside the first-floor window,
his father out there cursing the lack of parking spaces,
      his '34 Dodge rumbling without a tail

pipe. The super's daughter washing the vestibule stairs,
      everyone stepping over her bucket.
Mrs. White's cheeks flaming red she was so
embarrassed to be expired, white organdy like
      a cloud behind her head.

He knelt at the casket and asked forgiveness for feeling
      up her daughter. Mr. White standing
there like *My Man Godfrey* in a dark suit, greeting
everyone at the door, making proper introductions.
      Some of the kids coming on a dare,

touching her cold-meat hands. The women on folding
      chairs against the wall the same
women who sat outside on the sidewalk day after day,
under the locust tree, scolding him and his brother for
      fighting, before he went

to prison for holding up the drugstore with a switchblade.
      Before he was plastered on the front page
of *The Long Island Star*, dark hair mussed up, front tooth
chipped, a brother's shadow crossing his face. His father
      saying, "Let him get a taste of what it's really like."

THE LETTERS

He's moving into the darkness of an alleyway behind that woman's apartment, her packet of letters. She's everything he might have wanted, blonde in the middle of charcoal delineations. Tucked between red-ribboned correspondence, there's a tale of privilege, the long driveway, a summer estate, the yacht rocking at anchor, a man in white linen suit flashing wealth toward the heavens, the corpse of a girl at his feet. This man in the alley watching the girl's sister. Waiting her out. There she goes, bibbed uniform under her coat, living off tips in the diner, meals provided. Hard times, sick mothers, unbathed men slapped from the window by a night stick, what hasn't she seen. Dusk flicking its cassock. Pigeons staining streets. Late-morning light crumbling like aspirin.

It's dark still. He's opening her cardboard closet. Rifling her chest of drawers, cotton underwear caught on his fingertips, shaken off. He slides his hand over her naked absence, an album of photos. Two girls in the Adirondacks, their parents in a Model T, the brother who didn't come back from France—and if he had, the brother mowed down in tent city, the man spitting up his lungs. He hates it. The government. The men nobody can touch. He hates ferreting into and out of the light, his fedora like the promise of big-brained humans in the dawn. Here they are: the letters, the ribbon a strip of blood encircling cries that sounded like laughter, a throbbing speech that was escape, that named the lilac, the rose, the althea tree, the autumn crocus, a vase lifted to the moon. That's what wealth does. What one dies for. What he's sickened by, the mendacity of it, holding up the tissue of her little song. Remembering her twisted body. Her blackened lips.

He slips out into the city's combined shadows—slow text, sleepy narrative, the silence of falling light, emptiness in the last car of the elevated train like his office, where he's headed, where he arrives. Two rooms slashed by neon from across the street. His desk a careful clutter. Ashtray filled with shells of pistachio nuts. Stubbed-out Luckies. One of them lipstick-smudged. He's here in the dark, face flickering. Out of breath. The letters small and living in his hand, brought to his lair, to his hunger. He almost weeps. She lied. She must have written lies. And her sister, laying down coffee and pie this very minute, she listened. She listened in these letters to finches nesting in ivy crawling up a wall, the mansion wall, listened to a thrush singing in the deep wood, its throat pulsing in the grip of spring.

THE STROLL

It's happening again. Her daughter at school and she's walking
      naked down 28th Avenue. The sun
glancing off Sol's grocery window warms her nipples, the cool
Lifebuoy fragrance of her crazy-lady walk. Or maybe it's the taste
      of unfiltered fire she brings to her lips.

Mrs. Bakercy, Jerry's mother, rushing down with a blanket from
      her apartment over the candy store.
Sol's wife, quick to mark down on a paper bag what is owed,
calling the police. There's jeering from the barber leaning against
      his glassed-in twirling candy-stripe pole.

Sparrows scattering away from her shadow, a jabbering noise
      at her feet, where the mice in her kitchen
came to advise her. It's not her wild-eyed mother's warning
of a wobble in the cosmos. A dizziness just below the skin.
      This light-headedness is the breeze blowing

papers off a social worker's desk. The dive off a roof. Listen,
      she thinks, listen, her bare feet padding
on the cracked sidewalk in front of the French Cleaner's,
the steam press hissing in the rear, that's the sound of God
      coming up for air. She's walking past the movie

theater, the posters of rouged women who go all the way, their
      slick lovers as faded as last week's coming
attractions. That rubbing sound behind her is her daughter's eraser
wiping out a bad sum in P.S. 70 ten minutes before the milk break
      and her head on her arms for a nap.

CRIME

Crime is only the left-hand form of human endeavor, the lawyer says. The lawyer with the pencil-thin mustache. A gentleman's tie should always match his socks, he says. His wife plays cards in bed, begs him for a game of casino. Her sickness keeping her there. Her illness a state of mind, a perpetual belief in loss. Something he's also got to face, being broke. Two houses. Servants. Parties and champagne. Staying connected. A girlfriend on Front Street. But you know all that. You expected it, before anything was said, just like the hooligan's girl being thrown out of her room. She's coming up the stairs to ask him if she can stay. And he says, okay. Just don't get needy. Because he believes in loss too. The horse farm in Kentucky, acres of bluegrass gone. He just needs a big score. Then there's Doc, the professor, out after seven years, thinking of girls all the time. Looking at pinup calendars in the hack garage, waiting for a cab. All he needs is some working capital for a box man, a driver, a hooligan. The box man, the safe-cracker, with a sick kid and a worried wife. The driver a hunchback running a shabby little diner, a buddy of the hooligan.

All these men turned up by the bookie, who sweats day after day, his pockmarked face disappearing behind clouds of smoke like the moon. Who pays off Ditrich the plainclothesman to look the other way. And what they all need is below ground, in a vault, in a safe inside the vault, within velvet-lined trays, glittering even in the darkness, like the eyes of the hooligan's girl. Like the professor's palms. Like the clear ringing of alarms up and down the street. Like the shine on the .38 that falls out of the watchman's hand after the hooligan slugs him, that hits the ground and goes off, shooting the box man, who is laid out later in his two-room apartment with the priest gibbering over him, his wife holding the sick kid. Feeling nothing but loss. Then the lawyer tries a double cross and his private dick shoots the hooligan but gets shot himself. He's dead. The hooligan bleeding from his side. Now just the two of them running through the night, the professor and the hooligan. Trying to get to the hooligan's girl. Elsewhere, the lawyer's girlfriend crying in the apartment on Front Street, two cops next to her, when they hear the lawyer shoot himself. You knowing all this as if you were there, waking in a seedy room feeling a hot metal between you and the mattress, inhaling the burnt odor of events.

THE BOOKIE

You've come to expect it, accident and need smashing into each other like blind men in a ball room. Their dance empty of partners. Their milky eyes the dirty ice of comets that orbit the years with prophecy. All you need is an explanation on your behalf. Causes. The deliberate effect of a hand you can trust without seeing it or touching it. The odds you think about. He fiddles with cards, shuffling, reshuffling, taking bets, letting out news of a fix every now and then. You grab him by the collar and he squeals. He's the weak link. You slap him, alternating open palm and the back of your hand, back and forth, your arm a branch whipping in the wind. He's riding chance out of the gate, his head extended around the turn, his mouth puckering for luck's tit.

THE HUNCHBACK

It's easy to curse him because his looks are like deformed stories about the war, the flags, the women of New Guinea, all that hot greenery, the soldier with his stomach blown like a pudding, photos of girls back home soaked into the earth, the birds silent in the trees. He would have been there if he could. He would have taken the sniper's bullet that creased a friend's cheek. He would have saved the farm in Kentucky. Now he's made the anger in someone else's hands his own. Drives you into the darkness. Hides the score. Finds someone to conceal you from yourself. As if the law that twisted his back was the necessity of honor. And of love. And of choosing. And the law pursuing you was the family that allows no one to leave.

THE WIFE

Why is she always in bed, in her nightgown or street clothes? Is she coming or going? Why didn't she have any kids? You think an occasional game of cards with her husband is enough? You think he still wants her? She knows he doesn't. Then why does she want him? In another life, she'd be living in a furnished room. He'd be broke. She'd have a lover, who'd kill him. Which is why she cries so easily, knowing the loss of him happens one way or another. Something in the time that is her time clings like a mother's kiss. You keep wiping your cheek.

THE GIRL

The easy part is she's beautiful. Not so much dumb as single-minded. So whatever you say circles around and returns and goes out again and comes back, bound by her gravity. The fresh linen scent of her body changing into a fragrance of floribunda, peonies, honeysuckle, whatever's wild or plush or out of control. Whatever disappears in a day. Whatever takes the rent out of your hands at river's edge, casting shadows on the flow. Whatever makes her cry like a wife, when you say, "Just tell the truth."

THE PROFESSOR

If there's an explanation, he found it in solitary. All the pieces clicking into place. His accent a wisdom you never learned to mouth. He's boiling behind his eyes. He's got his hand on your shoulder. He's telling you who he doesn't trust, the noise of vehicles making him recoil, the jewel of his compressed thought glittering in your mind like a lesson you awaken to, sunlight sifting through dusty blinds, the girl packing up, telling you she's leaving.

As if you were on the verge of understanding it.

THE LAWYER

He's really a capitalist. Each woman an investment. And a responsibility. The glad hands of his youth aching. But look how many people depend on him. Between openness and the law, between a blow to the head and a caress, he's the thin gauze you see through, the texture of silky hopes, the argument a small boy once gave himself for keeping a found coin. Because opportunity is everywhere. Because the threadbare shirt tears into many rags, each wiping away a stain. Because the mist of the waterfront conceals the sound of running. Because hearing is blind to the gleam that must be stolen. Because explaining any of this is like looking inside a bird's throat for its song. A crumb passed from mouth to mouth. A cry of innocence. A rattling of chains.

THE OTHER WIFE

She knows the embrace of evening, the soft sounds of her child sleeping. She sits at the window, wondering if her husband is near. The cooked dinner cooling in the oven her day's offering to a God who has not yet brought him to harm. The cheap curtains with a valance lift in the breeze like a layer of light, like a thought of girlhood, like the frail fingers of her grandmother waving advice. "Never mind what he says. See what his heart is thinking." The nuns sent her forth and it was him or the sour weeping of a bereaved mother, querulous sisters. Him or the linty touch of the dry-goods store, the owner's unhemmed breath, the cold slide of change in her weekly envelope. Him or a tiny cubicle in which she asks hour after hour, "Number, please? Number, please?" Him or her own hand between her legs quietly rubbing.

The sound of two men coming up the stairs, carrying a burden.

THE OTHER GIRL

She's been a grown-up woman for years, bringing drinks to tables without spilling a drop. She'd be hard as nails, if the sun would just once not glare off the water and make her squint, keeping the world small. Maybe she's a little scared, not included in anyone's prayers, but not knocked up either, though she gives herself for the giving. One touch of her hand, you're afraid it's serious. Take the way her smile crooks up the left side of her mouth, almost in a sneer, and you know there's a box within a box, a light within a light, a seed within a seed. So when she comes running up the stairs because she's been thrown out of her place, you don't ask questions. You don't even have to believe what she says. She cleans up the kitchen—if you can call it a kitchen—and she makes the bed as if she'd never want to disturb it. And she says she's going to leave. So what makes her different? Why does the drinking glass seem to hum at her approach? Why does your emptiness begin to shine like crystal?

After *The Asphalt Jungle* (1950)

PAYOFF

CUTTING HIS WRIST

He was seven, cutting a hole in his new belt, twisting
    the point of the French carving knife
like an awl: mother sound asleep from her night shift
pushing up and down the brass handle of an elevator
    at the Astor Hotel; sinuses

filling with descent. Father snoring on his back from Tenth
    Avenue beer and a natural tendency
to get everything up his nose. The first day of the second grade,
weeks before he'd slide the knot of Tommy's tie up into his
    Adam's apple, choking him on

the front stoop because Tommy's mother stomped on their
    ceiling whenever they made a little
noise. Sister asleep in her crib, already behind the slats of a ward,
facing the wall. The future looped around him like a whip. Last
    week, he'd seen Sergeant York shoot

holes in foreheads from across a misty trench, mother coming
    to get him in the exploding dark. Now he
torqued that knife's honed hypotenuse gleaming like a swastika.
What did he know of evil? All he wanted was to keep his knickers
    high, argyle socks in place, his golfer's

stance the envy of Mrs. Thompson in her fur coat that he stroked
    during fire drill. Then his wrist spurted
red flame. Arterial blood. The entire reach of his lungs grabbing
at the severed belt, lips opening below his grasp. He ran into the
    bedroom, uplifted hand, splashed throat,

blond hair, all of him fleeing. Father leaped out of bed. Mother
        pumped an unseen
handle to get them out of there. Sister stared with liquid eyes
to melt the heart of death. You can see the scar threading
        the radial knob to the flex of my palm

when I make dog shadows on the wall. It wrinkles like the skin
        on sauce left to cool
uncovered in the air. Dry as the scrape of a window opening.
Rough as the sewed lips of zombies tottering through Steinway
        Street's movies. Something half-born.

GLARE

In all this San Jose light there is not a shadow on the patio near the pool, not a thin line of darkness on formica counters in the kitchen, her indoor balcony staring over flawless white tile floors and the walls hung with ivory animals. The bullet speeding from her long-nosed revolver travels in the pale surf sound tearing down into his sternum, his stomach, blasting his liver. Even as her arm drops to her side, the sun moves to prevent the memory of it, such dazzle the glister of a thousand children opening their eyes. It's like walking on polished marble in her bare feet, sliding over its coolness, as his dark distorted mouth loses its fondness for shaping lies. There is no one working on the grounds, scooping the pool, vacuuming a floor. No garbage disposal. No dust. No sign of a cat or dog.

A thin, transparent breeze continues without a particle of soot. The throbbing of an engine is the heat of her thighs and light opens like a shriek that cannot be heard in the deaf valley below, the hills surrounding the estate just the broken-off legs of giants who have not survived their time. She has no past to remember. And whatever he did has been erased before it ever happened, before the sweet leaves opened from their buds and there were picture books in bed and someone humid with lilac read Aesop's fables to that girl as deep within her pillow as a dark-eyed nestling unlidding its gaze.

CONFESSION

Maybe there were worse things than cutting off some fool
      making a left turn on 28th Avenue,
anger a cool stone basin he could dip into. Patricia Farrel
pouting behind her hat's veil on Easter Sunday, resurrection
      a real lift while his father

was breathing glassy-eyed in bed, milky women stepping off
      the covers of crime novels on the night
table. The priest's leaky voice hissed through the screen.
Forgiveness smelled like rose water on fingers he lifted to his
      nostrils. Outside, the rumble

of souped-up Fords. Their black fender skirts a grace on rainy
      nights, trapping the slop of
wheels. Penance in the Saturday night bath, where he could
scrub away the twitch of Mary Biloti's skirt or submerge his head
      not to hear her laughter unraveling

down the stairs from where she lived on the top floor, breasts
      budding in a jail-bait mohair sweater.
The body a kingdom of narrow roads, shaggy white horses
surging through the evening, a balding gnomish man slapping
      the reins, snapping his whip,

and inside the coach a sailor back from the war, finger-fucking
      his girl, her groans louder than
the hooves pounding the road. He's trying to read on the broken-
spring couch in the living room away from siblings, the crowded
      bedroom, his father snoring,

Annie across the hall sneaking out of her parents' apartment
        to catch the bus on Steinway Street, a late movie
in Manhattan, gartered nylon thighs rubbing against each other
as she passes the door, his headlights half-lidded with silver,
        exhausts mumbling, his hand ready to accelerate.

GAS STATION

Travel meant opening a Buick hood from the side, scraping
      my knuckles on the radiator,
toeing down the accelerator pedal to start the engine. I took
the credit cards that Moses Brown couldn't read, and wrote in
      addresses from New Jersey,

Illinois, Kansas. Sometimes, the hatcheck girl came in with her
      Plymouth convertible, showing
plenty of leg as I filled her up. Last week, a man knocked his girl
out with a lug wrench and she lay next to the pumps, blouse open,
      her breasts stopping traffic. I watched her wake up,

just walk away. I wrote the names of all the women I knew who
      I wanted to lie there on the ground without
covering up and circled three. Every Saturday, a man came selling
condoms in glittering foil out of a suitcase, talking about his days
      in California. Endless sun. Starlets in the Cherokee

Hotel. The cheapness of the Hollywood Y. When he left, the sky
      darkened over the Hudson River. Cars backed up
from the entrance to the Lincoln Tunnel. No one could get in
for gas. Moses poured whiskey into paper cones and the two
      of us quaffed eighty proofs of our effectiveness.

PAYOFF

The policy for the husband's car. The husband busy in the oil fields. The maid out for the afternoon. The wife at the top of the stairs, refracting light in the insurance salesman's eyes where he stands in the tiled entryway, prickling to her shattered-glass voice, a cubist flow to her descent, the naked smoke of her cigarette. He doesn't ask if she loves her husband's slippery hands, now not in the study while he's looking at her ankle bracelet, legs bare under a white skirt, his hand with its swimmer's bleached knuckles resting on the rich wood table, next to the policy, while he talks about actuarial x's of suicide: the leap out the window, off the cliff, off the bridge; warm wrists reddening the bath. "Who's talking of suicide?"

But he goes on. Disgust or vanity surmised in head-shot. Heart-shot. "Never mind murder." "Who's talking of murder?" His hand brushes against the policy, paragraphs written on water—a wavering text for fathers who tuck in children, who count bales in the field, who load trucks all night and drive home trying not to stare into oncoming lights, who don't hire nurses to pull blankets off a sick wife, who don't snarl at the nurses after the funeral, after they marry them and complain about the money spent on hats, the capes, the open-toe shoes and square-shoulder dresses, the gold anklet reading, "Fuck Me, I'm Yours."

But the air coming through the study window she opens is honeysuckle. Her husband in the oil fields. The maid off for the evening bringing groceries to a mother somewhere downtown. The step-daughter out with a boyfriend who can't hold a job as a soda jerk, who's angry even before he was born, before his father can't speak English, who drops out of the Graduate Equivalency Diploma course before it stales, who can't learn the computers that haven't been invented yet, who's lost on the Web before it becomes invisible. Who'll get blamed.

But that won't work because when they're in the A&P, the salesman and the wife talking back to back like strangers looking at the canned corn and baby potatoes and French string beans, after the husband's been bludgeoned and thrown off a train, years before HUAC is asking their actor friends what meetings they were attending when Fuchs gave up the bomb, before all the cars had blinking directionals, before skirts fell below the knees, before the sun bled on the Yalu River, before poets made money on madness, before wives stayed home wearing little aprons and stood tiptoe to kiss tall husbands, before you could see nakedness on the screen or even say "boo," the salesman and the new widow in the produce section of the store that will expand in ten years to the size of a barn, they keep reaching for the same loaf of enriched white bread, their hands touching in the brightly lit aisle like doves that flutter close, then part, and any damn fool can see the investigator watching them from behind the cans of evaporated milk, his face gleaming between the pictures of cows.

After *Double Indemnity* (1944)

THE HAT, THE TIE

THE HAT, THE TIE

They were chums from the same private school when fathers drove up in roadsters with mistresses. Now, one friend's in New York. The other in Argentina, a sculptor. He comes back north, because he's always wanted the friend's wife, even before he went to South America. He tries not to think about her in her husband's arms, his hands trembling.

The husband's got a pencil-thin mustache, theater tickets, waiting at the bar, from the very start waiting, thinking he'll call Buenos Aires for a chat. He knocks back two martinis, unable to figure out if there are one or two women in the story. Two if you count the woman this very minute sitting next to him at the bar. Later, there'll be three. His wife dead already. He doesn't know that. So just say three women. He slumps over his drink. The sadness of it all. The mystery.

The friend turning his hands this way and that. Eye-twitch rippling his cheek. Light slashing into headaches. Pulling on white gloves, snapping a necktie taut, looking down at the wife, words flying into his face, taunting. Because that's what love is. Torture.

The woman next to the husband at the bar—her hat tilts on her head, a galactic swirl seen edge-on, giving off a plume of stellar dust. A really sad woman, without name or address. But she helps the husband use the tickets his wife isn't coming for, goes to the musical, because she can be alone even sitting next to him like a wife, nodding at the drummer who ogles her over his traps, over the *tim-tim* of his hi-hat clapping—as if he knows her. Behind him, on stage, the Latin singer, the woman kicking out her bare legs, wearing the same hat as the woman with the husband, glaring at her across the lights, the woman staring back. The hat a huge stepped-on pastry, a bad taste in the mouth, a lying lover's kiss, the drummer's *ping-a-ping*.

The friend, the sculptor, carves big heads in white marble, obvious heads, monumental heads. He's clawing his face, his headache like one of the huge heads trying to burst out.

The husband's only alibi is in seeing the woman in the hat. He could say he was there looking at her, she was being seen, and therefore so was he, even though she came out that evening to be invisible. Sometimes, only the drummer is looking and the hat is a great black saucer blocking the light, like the shades pulled down in the friend's apartment, a man's silk tie just a drawstring, just a way of bringing darkness into a woman's eyes.

The woman in the hat almost not there later, saying good-by, shaking the husband's hand. The drummer looking back and forth—the two hats, the brash, split-skirt singer and the mournful woman, how could the same hat belong to both?

The husband comes home to the dark apartment. Three cops waiting inside, one of them in his favorite chair. She's in the bedroom, the wife, her face covered with a sheet, so you can't see the color of her hair. The clothes hanging in the closet, nothing that would go with the hat. The tie twisted so tight around her neck it has to be peeled off. The husband's tie. A shop on Fifth Avenue, the elderly salesman with a British accent, he could say when he bought it. But this doesn't matter because the sculptor bought one there also, on the same day. Not meaning to follow him. Not wanting to. He really does look like the husband. Without a mustache. The way they sat next to each other in Classics, parsing the *Iliad*, the teacher not knowing one from the other. But this is not the same as the hat, where the women don't know each other and the trait they share is some staticky accident of motion and cool air and carpeting. Their paths crossing at random. They both liked that hat, one of them sad, the other singing and pumping her pelvis on stage. But not like the two halves of one woman, because there's a third. The wife. There's always more.

The tie. The detective drapes it across his hand. The sculptor wearing one just like it. He's shown up without being phoned. But he forgets which one he used, which one came from the husband's closet, both of them slung over his forearm that time. As if it wouldn't matter which was which, laid out as evidence. What everything comes to. Loving her. The husband with his face buried in his hands. The agency of these events somewhat in the hat connecting the sad woman to the husband losing his wife. The emblem of a forsaken world. Why witnesses can't be found. The sculptor lying to his friend, which is almost worse than screwing his wife, saying he was in South America.

When he wasn't.

After *Phantom Lady* (1944)

INSURANCE

ON THE CUFF

Mark it down. The Mueller's Spaghetti loose in its box.
     The White Rose Peas. The Quaker
Oats pincered down from the top shelf. In the long column
of numbers, subtract his father two weeks out sick, his sister's
     abscessed tooth, her face

swollen like a melon. Add the Yankee Doodles and the soft
     cream inside everything,
the can of Puss 'n' Boots cat food that smells like low tide
and the dark mud near La Guardia Airport, where his bike
     snapped its front fork

and he nearly tumbled into the path of a bus. Don't forget
     the eggs, the Campbell's
Tomato Soup, the pale blood in the lower eyelid. Or the Duz
that rinses out gray. Or after the Saturday matinee, after the
     matron's flashlight

lit his face, don't forget Tetley's tea on the way home, or how
     long it will take
this day's total to matter in the million sums that glitter
in the grocer's eyes, a man once chased into an alley in Berlin
     and almost burned alive.

BRIBE

It's true he hid from the cops, but first, here's what he did.
     Drunk and smashing his son's
Ford coupe into a parked car and then leaving it in the street
alongside the Loew's Triboro, where Orson Welles plays a
     cop so bad the fortuneteller says,

"Your future's all used up." He runs upstairs to his apartment,
     not telling his wife what happened,
and gets into bed and tries to sleep it off, but the cops follow him
and he tells them to wait for his son. Because he's not really
     allowed to drive a car. He's got a special

license for driving only a truck because he had an accident last
     year and didn't have insurance
and couldn't post a bond. He can't lose that license and lose his
living, see. The coupe with a crunched fender sitting in the street,
     the cops waiting for the son to come home

from his night classes. Holding the keys. Suddenly, a guy pulls out,
     so they push the coupe
into a parking space. They hang out in the diner across the way,
where I amble in for a burger and coffee, my head full of *Macbeth*,
     the wife with red hands, the person they tell you

is really to blame, putting bad ideas in your head. I'm worried
     about History, why things happen, I'm in a fog,
wondering why all these cops are here, until I get home and you
know what I hear from my mother. I go back to the diner and ask
     for the keys to my car. I slip the cop ten bucks,

so he fills in a report saying that I did it. He tells me to wait on the
    corner. A cop car pulls up, the cop swinging the keys
from his finger inside the car. I reach in and drop another ten and
say, "I took care of the other guy." I get the coupe going and park
    it somewhere else, I go upstairs.

I find my father, covers pulled up to his chin like a baby. "Those
    fuckin' cops!" he says. "I took care of them," I say.
He smiles. The first time I ever did something he admires.
"Those fuckin' cops!" I feel really good for the first time in weeks,
    my name not just a scribble on a page.

INSURANCE

My father and his mother dying on the same day miles apart,
　　the faint sonar of their failing
brains pinging through the air of Long Island, crisscrossing
the Grand Central Parkway like a song trying to find its
　　way. Now this old man sitting

in the kitchen after the double wake, my mother asking, "Guess
　　who this is?" It's *her* father,
florid, paunchy, telling me how he drove an ambulance in WWI
across muddy fields and got gassed. Why he coughs so much.
　　All the years later, after he disappeared?

"You were better off without me." The youngest child given away?
　　Stolen? "She's probably an actress somewhere."
Eyes a bleary blue like sky in a pond, he looks at his daughter.
"Did he leave you much?" I remembered a thin scream coming
　　from my father, when my mother, without a dime, let

the union dues lapse. Insurance lost. Sun trying to get through
　　the curtained window. The borrowed air conditioner
blowing a coolness into the sick man's bedroom like the breeze
I felt coming off the desert in a Maria Montez movie, her lover
　　galloping all night to save her from the snake worshipers.

LUNG

There it was, 1950-something, his right lung a little weak, verging
    on exhaustion in the evening high
school class, in the middle of a history exam, fluttering uncertainly
as he imagined Roosevelt leaning over at Yalta, Stalin smirking
    because he could see FDR fading in the blown-back

smoke of Churchill's cigar. But there was an hour to go and other
    essays to write. Africa. The American
Constitution. The lung went suddenly limp as an empty pajama
sleeve spread out on the bed. He looked up at the smeared black-
    board and remembered Chekhov at Yalta spitting up

blood, looking like Paul Muni playing Emile Zola, ogling women.
    In present time, the lung just couldn't get any
attention, swelling now like a sigh trying to escape from a book.
It began to curl like a manta ray riffling the ends of its body
    as it slid deeper into the bottom currents

of a tropical sea. No question it was hiding. He was breathing
    hard, heart pounding, two jobs taking a toll—
at home a father drinking up a storm. The lung fluttered and went
sailing into the ribs of an eerie white wreck. He gasped. Africa,
    500 words. It tried so hard not to flatten like drapes

pulled shut to block the air, not to shrink from the glare of Mau
    Maus, the stink of wiped machetes, the stiff gaze of
the teacher. Not to find itself beneath a sterterous father rolling
over in bed every night onto a wife. It wanted to just collapse.
    Or step out into the star-struck night for a little breeze.

LOSING THE TAKE

Trouble is, sometimes I'm the disoriented little man with a rifle and stained teeth and narrow head in the race-track parking lot. I'm facing the wrong way when the horses come round the turn and the wrong horse wins, the filly I never got a bullet into. There's no pile-up, no confusion. The police remain at their posts in the counting room, when I break in wearing a latex hobo mask that shudders when they rip it off. I grow a cop's face. I get away.

But there's no argument over splitting the take that hasn't been snatched and no bullet travels through someone's lung or cracks the glassed picture of Atlantic City. I don't have to go down on my knees before my wife while she's packing her bags to run away with her boyfriend. She has to stay in the two-room apartment, the walls closing in, the noise of traffic rising to the mouth of her window, the acrid exhaust of the cars forever at the light. She tosses on the daybed's soiled sheets, crying, "It eats me alive!"

Sometimes I dream of a young wife bending over in her house dress. Or I'm taller, I'm the boyfriend caught by the woman's bookkeeper husband next door, and I shoot the squirt. I jump the woman again and again. She digs nails into my arm and screams for more. Sometimes I remember the crazy idea from the race-track bartender with the looker wife, that we go into business with a snacks concession truck, wear white Nedick's caps and drive from factory to factory with shelves of Danish pastries and ham sandwiches. Chumps for life.

I dream I'm living in a trailer on the edge of the desert, my wife complaining about her dry throat and the small bullet hole in my head from the robbery, when was it, Jesus, almost before Roosevelt died and it still hasn't healed.

After *The Killing* (1956)

THE TAKE

THE ASPHALT JUNGLE II

The first thing to know is that its value changes. Maybe it's all that time you spend believing the years are a corridor you squeeze through, your shoulders scraping against what you've been told and what is really given, the crime of it being the dimness ahead. And if you bump into something at your feet, if you break it open and it looks like something everyone wants, and you can remember a time when no one asked you for anything at all, then there must be someone in Chicago or New York who would pay double for it. Who'd make you feel good. Who'd buy back the mortgage you entered the world with. And everything stupid would be like a man in an expensive suit, flicking ashes on the carpet that isn't yours. You don't care. But will it buy back your grandfather's acres, if you get only half of real worth? Is it the spark and splitting of light or just the hard edge etching glass that the lawyer argues will make the difference for all of you? One an appearance that blinds you in a restaurant lit by candles, paling the romantic light, brighter than the flash in your eyes at interrogation. The other a sharp heft, a cold reasoning, a snicked boundary, a perfectly divided life, so that when you step over a threshold, there's an immediate warmth, the sound of children running, a table set for dinner. And behind you a whirl of papers, soot in the street, someone blowing a whistle, cop cars zigzagging like lit cigarettes in the dark. The only transgression being that if you turn away once, it's too late to turn again.

THE DETECTIVE

Everyone knows he takes a buck to look the other way. But the heat is on. The commissioner will have him back pounding a beat unless he gets results. All the peddlers, produce men and candy store owners will be pressing can openers, pears, chocolates into his hand, his luck melting away. The bookie's little bundle of cash will dry up like dog piss. There'll be no blonde on the sofa afraid of him. He won't know anything anymore. He'll be back to start, unable to name the shapes that pass. That nod his way. That slip an envelope into his mouth to stop his talking.

THE BLACK COLT

If nature were that friendly, he wouldn't be kicking his rear legs into the air. The rot of barns and poorly drained meadows would be cool as an apse on Easter morning. The mended paddocks would unheal themselves. There'd be long acres for him to run and run.

THE COMMISSIONER

He's in charge through no right of his own. Not born to it, not filled with light on the road to somewhere. Only a suited bureaucrat behind a desk. Only angry. Only flailing the law over your head, as if something essential could be driven out of you, as if conscience were a tufted seed carried on the wind all the way to the river, an excessive current sweeping it along. And when he demands that you present yourself, that you give yourself up, that you confess where you succeeded, there is only a darkness that keeps you pinned against a wall, footsteps making you hold your breath, as if getting caught were a matter of fatigue with concealment. Inadequate insight. Because law is everywhere and immeasurable. Because each escape makes everything worse.

THE HOOLIGAN

Here's the infinite regress of money, blame, accidental death, collapsed risk, greed, a banker's dry smile, a deed folded twice, the cash accounts, the first forty acres sold, ten of them transformed from bluegrass to crops, the grown colt's broken leg, the vet's pistol shot, his mother's seamed face a plowed field, the fruit of capital fallen, bruised, a brownish waste in his mouth, a woman who once loved him, who wrote once to the soldier, once to the jailbird he became, before he never returned, anger now a skill, injury coming to him like a fragrance out of the Kentucky woods, something he nurtures, what he recognizes in others, the small light that grows smaller in the eyes, as if the enemy he killed for country took into a shallow grave the guiltless inflections of his seeing, each gas station, each grocery store, each coffee shop knocked over like mannequins in a window, not the real thing.

THE PROFESSOR

He'll explain it to you. First, there are repetitions, which is why you've done time. Second is the carelessness you bring to events, as when the bookie asks you to pay up, and you're insulted, because welshing is a sign of cowardice, and you always see a thing through to its end. Third is the ache and itch of companionship. Fourth is the sudden image of sky with drifting clouds that interrupts your thoughts. Fifth is the fear of being remembered. Sixth is the anger at being forgotten. Seventh is the way you drag your life along. Eighth is the way you try to name it. Ninth is the way you display it to others. Tenth is the feeling of usefulness when someone cringes at your approach. Eleventh is the memory of music from an open window. Twelfth is the way you raise yourself up and never ask forgiveness.

THE LAWYER

You'd think he'd be a good judge of his own chances and yours. The social thinker, the opportunist, the deal-maker who balances the scales and brings joy to everyone, sipping a martini. That's what a man's pockets are for, he says, where things of the world slide home.

Every absence attracting a fullness. One man's loss, another's gain. In this way, too, his women profit. Why did his wife allow her own largesse to be squandered? Style, he did it all with style. For the sake of style. For the look in everyone's eyes. For the surfaces that catch the early morning light as if they had inherent brightness. Advantage is what he offers, like the fence who gives you less for more, who takes your name out of it, the take you carry with you of no value in and of itself. Everything brokered by desire. By his ringed hands. The value of what you hold divided by profit or disgrace, honor or salaciousness, gentility or the raw smell of blood. As if the bowels of the earth were chrome, and what opens to view is the hum of equipment, the purged body, precise cause and effect, all of it tuned to his telephone dial as he makes the call. As he betrays. And the sickness you sense within yourself is just what the Professor predicted. Corruption on the wind. The wrongness that pursues you like a god's arrows now just the feeble impingement of the bookie's weeping. The collapse of odds.

THE GIRL

Not that she has no life of her own. The clothes he bought her, hanging in the closet, the negligees, the soft, fluffy slippers, the perfumes on the dresser, the rented living-room furniture, the down mattress she will let him watch her sleeping on, without touching, are only transparent promises, only what *he* requires. When he asks her to lie to the cops, when he draws her forth from a glassy world, she brings warmth to his fear. She wants to do the right thing. The lost years of high school, the stepfather's icy hand under the blanket, a mother's disbelief, the boiled face of the priest, the shame of thought itself, what is conspiracy to these, if she is both herself and not? If the silk shine of her hips is the stray brilliance of memory? Hope in the beholder's eye? The air vibrant with truth? That faint sound the unlatching of the revolver's safety catch in the other room?

THE WIFE

Always she sits in bed waiting to be told where he is. Always she is never told. Always he never arrives. Always the accounts are lacking funds. Always the servants begin to leave. Always she begins to learn where the important papers are. Always there is a chill in her finger-tips from something pressing on her spine. Always a niece calls to arrange a visit. Always someone is pressing the bell at the front door. Always the conjugation of rain and sadness makes her think of his nervousness. Always the years of travel to Mexico, Paris, Rio, London are the itineraries of sleep. Always the ghost of his touch roams over her body like someone examining his belongings. Always she imagines herself driving down the hill, along the sea, into the heat shimmer of a vast, level road.

Lost and beginning to like it.

THE PROFESSOR AND THE JUKEBOX

The girl and her boyfriends dancing around it like a volatile, sacred thing, her skirt swirling, half the take glittering in his briefcase, while he forgets the last days in Berlin, the yellow star sewn to his coat, the history of then. But you know all that. You expect her beauty, her youth, her bright acceptance of his nickels when the boys go broke, to be why his mind has rid itself of everything else. The natural drift of money, the surplus of labor, the warmth outside the dankness of his cell, everything surmised from the simplest rhythms of the sun. His hesitation the acceptance of being caught. The long, fine chain of circumstances that have led to this moment. His freedom in the way the girl does not deny him. And anything he might have to say already foreknown, except in the way he believes he has only himself to blame, as if the passing of minutes seethed in their passage, fumed, obfuscating the seasons, his wisdom a matter of inches, clarity a drop of rain already misshapen as it slides down a window.

THE OTHER GIRL

Maybe she was the girl in the back row in third grade who liked you. Who matched you sum for sum, word for word, in all the stand-up quizzes, your teacher widowed from the war staring at the both of you. The best in class. Almost the same height. Almost pals. The one you never kiss. The one who brings you to the fields you've never seen, holding a rag to your wound. Through the scrim of her long hair, where she bends over you, you watch the world fade. You inhale regret like the odors of hay and manure, from the city under the city. But she'll be there when you rise again. She's already waving from the other side. She was here in this place even when you turned around to see her smile in the back row. She was here waiting, while you saw through her in class, through the time to come, through the slide of fallen manacles, through the lit rain on paved streets, the long, slow wail of sirens the call of her blood. The knowing of what was missed.

After *The Asphalt Jungle* (1950)

DETOUR

DRIVING WITH BOHDAN HAMERSKY

We've done it, dropped out of school, out of our Broadway jobs,
      driving a '56 DeSoto to L.A.
for some guy in North Hollywood, our first stop Dayton, Ohio,
the rooms at the Y just bins, chicken wire across the top, as if
      we're in a holding pen, waiting

to get booked. "You sleeping?" "Nah." Plywood walls—we've
      talked through worse. Cots white as bandages.
Fries steaming in our guts. The desk clerk's Philco portable
playing Big Band stuff. Maybe we're in the wrong time. Maybe
      Dan will wake up back in Vienna, his father

just stabbed in an alley. "They followed him," he says. His
      father always on his mind, a hero
who resisted the Nazis, then the Commies. Listen, I'll take the
movies. Orson Welles on that Ferris wheel, telling his friend
      everyone's out to make a buck. Except Dan

and me. Three one-hundred-dollar bills in my pocket like love
      letters from our girls waiting for us in Malibu.
Or is it Sunset and Vine? Next night, Moline, Illinois, a Short
Subject that's gone on too long. When does it turn, when do you
      stop twisting on a lumpy mattress? When is it not

a rerun? Dan driving today on the flat roads of Nebraska, the Y
      in Omaha clean as a church. We go
to a crummy picture about couples buying little Spic and Span
homes, windows that spy on each other, wives getting undressed
      for the mechanic next door to see

what he's missing. If we wanted *that*, we'd have stayed at our
          part-time jobs wearing brown usher uniforms
with braid on the collars like the lacy hems of the talky ladies
on stage, night after night. I mean, what's real? What's debt?
          Who do you owe?

So we whoop it up in Denver, courage a little thin on the
          mountain road to Salt Lake City,
that religion so buoyant you're always rising. Dan's studying
to be an architect. He sizes up a room the way you study
          a map, finding the dead ends. Looking

for the opening to the sea. This last chance, before he's in
          that movie. We can't wait to get to Las Vegas.
A million bucks in the casino window. Slot machines even
next to the toilets. Neon chances lighting up our nerves
          like the fingertips of beautiful women.

DETOUR

The only difference between him and Oedipus is Oedipus didn't slouch over black coffee in a roadside diner and whimper and drive everyone nuts playing bluesy music on the juke, after he did what he did, road dust filling the seams in his leather jacket. All he wants is to reach Hollywood, his girl, the singer tired of gigs in smoky bars and the stink of everyone else's fate. She took the next Greyhound out. But okay, he killed a stranger on the road, who gave him a lift, who was bleary on pills, who let him drive the convertible like it was a two-man chariot with a team of black horses. There wasn't anyone who didn't stare at the push-button doors, the spare on the outside of the trunk like a life preserver, wide-band whitewalls spinning backward even though the car is moving forward, because that's how motion is when everything gets accomplished before it gets started. And how you tell it to sweaty faces at the police station.

Maybe Oedipus's father also fell out on the passenger side and hit his head on a stone. Wouldn't Oedipus have taken his wallet before he rolled him into the scrub, not wanting to waste a perfectly good identity, suddenly somebody with a wife and son, his name a shower of static up and down the highway?

He's driving in the rain and can't get the top in place, then he picks her up, bedraggled, hair plastered to her head, eyes sunken and crazed, her smile like a knot being tied. She knows this car. She's been in it before, when its owner gave her a ride and reached between her legs. Into her mystery. And she raked him. (A wound seen by our man in the very beginning, when the owner popped pills—thick fingers, the rings, scabs like sunspots on the backs of his hands, the manager of every joint two lovers ever played in, giving our man a ride.)

She laughs at his eyes fixed on the white line, hot to arrive, as if his whole life wasn't already absent, and hers not still trapped somewhere in a furnished room, the picture on the bureau not her parents but models that come with a frame. She's like the Sphinx, taking his measure, nobody to faint over. This is no coincidence. The driver, the sap, she tells him she knows what he did. Look at him sweat. Look at his piano-player's hands squeezing the wheel. She sidles up to him, to his riddle, the big jewel, a kind of stash in his stories about the girl. His dumb-shit loyalty.

Later, in the motel suite, under the phony married name, she passes out drunk in a locked room, telephone cord around her neck. He's in the other room, wanting to call his girl in Hollywood, and he pulls the cord under the door. He hauls in the future, hand over hand, making it happen, coiling it around her throat, until she's lying dead with a wine-dark mouth, the trapped syllables of his name frozen in her eyes.

He's telling this to a perfect stranger in a roadside diner. Everyone turns away. The truck driver is leaning over the neon juke. The muzzy waitress shoves across the coffee black and swirling like the story he can't drag himself out of. He's sweaty, smudged, moaning about the love song the truck driver buys for a lousy nickel.

Then it flips. It turns. He imagines himself arriving a hero in L.A., outside his girl's home, where she's been singing him all this way, her white dress a field of snow in the land of sun. Something washes up a wreck inside him. She's waiting for his call, for his voice to dive at her through the wire. All she has to do is pull her knitting close, sweep the entryway clear of cops, keep something cold in that old refrigerator with the coils humming on top. All she needs is the sound of him driving up, a jingle of keys, a battered suitcase full of stories rubbing against his stained and shiny pants, his kingly smile shining down on prints of road dust left by his feet on a broken walkway.

After *Detour (1945)*

CULVER CITY

He took out *The Sorrows of Young Werther* from the little Public
      Library and dreamt he was flying
over the East River, scattering last words like feathers. Here,
among trees on the fenced-off movie lot, cowboys rear on black
      horses, the film grinds on. The train that runs through

town is erased from the sound track, like everything he used
      to be. At work, the Japanese woman speaks of her
internment during the war, lost identities, spraying red lacquer
on white plastic, making parts bleed in the sun. All he hears at
      night is the whisper of falling syllables.

Sometimes an irritation of friends, their letters a protest against
      travel, unvarying warmth, weather that draws no
line. He stands outside the margin. Known facts a wobbly
shimmer on the road, the '47 Dodge's stiff steering a way of
      getting into downtown L.A. that promises

no easy return. Friday night, the only movie theater in Culver
      City shows science fiction, creatures
that breathe blue gas. All weekend he smells acrid traces
all around him, until the landlady knocks on his cottage door,
      early and fragrant for rent.

THE PICTURE

1

This is before you get to me shot through the head. Clouds racing across the moon. I'm strolling somewhere in the shadows off Malibu, smoking a gold-tipped cigarette, life evaporating like sweet aftershave from my cheeks. There's nothing I haven't done.

The Author driving around town in a banged-up coupe, visiting editors who finger his scripts. All they want is the upbeat ending. A little romance. They make him sick to his stomach.

Next day I'm at my girlfriend's home, arguing with her chauffeur about the mud spattered on her husband's Packard. I know I'm being watched by a private dick, and I look up over the hedge along the driveway at the dented Mercury parked down the street, the dick smoking a fancy cigarette, taking notes.

I laugh. The photo I took, they want it. I thought it was just the long legs of the drum majorette, the high-school band marching past, the Fourth of July like any other hot day. I thought I was just horny, snapping my Kodak, drooling over the kid's gams. Just feeling happy, until this old man falls out of the window. And I get a picture of how it really happens.

The Author stubs out his cigarette in the ashtray in the Mercury that smells like a flophouse. He's bored with this character who thinks he's on his own, Mr. Slick. He's tired of keeping an eye on him. As if he didn't have other clients in a jam. Wasn't in one himself. The world needs new ideas. He starts reading a newspaper, going over old stories, trying to get a little history into his thinking,

and me, I'm looking over the hedge, I see him reading, as if he's waiting for someone to get off a bus. Someone to show himself. My girlfriend sprawled in sunlight, next to the pool, calls to me and I feel small, like a mint rolling around in her mouth.

2

The sky gets hazy. The neighborhood around me begins to waver in heat shimmer, as if it's going to disappear, as if enough evil has accumulated and the world is ending, all my art objects falling off their shelves at home. All my scams. I'm scared. I look up over the hemlocks for the faded Mercury in the street, the driver with hat brim snapped down. But there's no one there. I flick the butt out of its holder, insert a fresh Benson & Hedges.

The Author in his shabby office, staring at his typewriter, remembering the charge he led in the Great War. His wife not well, twenty years his senior, beginning to gray and sag, a long time out of a best friend's bed.

The Author heaving up his breakfast in the hallway toilet.

The Author remembering how his wife played the piano. Her beautiful hands. Her class. How she cries herself to sleep.

He thinks what he wants to do to me. Something harsh. Something cruel.

3

Whether the secretary pushed the old man out the window during the parade, or his wife did, I've been putting the arm on both the widow and the secretary, who thought they could just push the old man out of their lives. I figure he must have been fondling the secretary, a girl out of the Midwest, just a kid, and the wife sees this. How much longer does she have to wait for him to die anyway? I've seen their house, the pillars in front, the servant, the leather chairs, the two cars, the smell of money, probably a screwed-up son who can't pay his gambling debts, can't take care of himself. Can't keep his hands off the secretary either. What a crew.

I don't know the half of it and I'm rolling in dough. The dick they hired can't do anything about it.

The chauffeur splashes me with the hose. We argue. Vera waves me over to the pool for a kiss. "C'mere."

We kiss.

"What's wrong with you?"

"I think I caught a chill."

4

I'm drinking a lot. Maybe the dick is really working for Vera's husband. Today I'm following the Mercury. I'm bored sleeping with another man's wife, trapped in someone else's habit. Sometimes in the dark her voice strange, the feel of her wrong, in the morning those gold hairs glinting on the pillow like something synthetic. What's the point, when you don't feel like yourself anymore? I mean it's taking me back to childhood, as if I got lost there. And when I go looking in the past, every room is empty. There's no one in the park. No cars parked along the river. The wind like an eraser wiping away detail. As if I never existed. So how could I be sleeping with anyone's wife? And if someone fell from a window, it's like a piece of asteroid falling through space. No one sees it, it doesn't happen. Maybe that picture I took made the old man fall. So when I'm seeing anything I'm making it up, I'm causing it. It wouldn't be there if I wasn't there. Sure they want that photo. Once it's gone, I'm gone. Nothing ever happened. No one could ever lie about it. Or is it once I'm gone, it's gone? Get rid of me or the photo, it's the same thing. The son gets the secretary. The wife gets peace of mind.

I see where the Mercury parks, the dick tilted to one side as he walks, his fedora greasy where he's always creasing it with his fingers. I feel something pinching my spine. I watch sunlight roll off him like a darkness. I go into the building, into the elevator and talk to the geezer whose uniform smells like a cold mothball.

A five-spot and he tells me about the dick's high-class accent, the guy's scar from some ditch in France. Silk ties. The Latin book under his arm. The smell of booze. He's been a wreck a long time, the dick. Who the hell would believe in him? I give him the negative and he gives it to those women and they pay him off and he walks away and I got nothing. It's not right. None of this helping me going up and up. I feel dizzy. I'm stepping away from myself, out of the cage. I'm thinking, get this guy off your back.

I feel a breeze coming out of the side of my head.

5

The Author hasn't eaten for days, slugging back Seagram's, drumming his fingers, working the story in a fever. Truth tossing and turning. A kind of loneliness exhaling from his Royal typewriter. Someone's silhouette appears in the frosted glass panel of his door. Someone knocks. You can't tell if it's me or not, because the shade is

drawn, there's not enough light in the doorway to read your name by.
He's sitting there looking at his hands under the desk lamp.

Later, a woman leaves the office who was never seen entering it.

6

I've been shot through the temple. I'm hanging over the back of my davenport, dead eyes staring at my own decor, head swung back, ogling the pictures on my wall, watercolor trees, a misty lake upside down, as if I was just remembering childhood, the whistle of a train cutting through Long Island, past the bathers at Ronkonkoma, past my sister in the ward at Creedmoor, all the way to Queens. As if some woman had been listening to me talking about that, and all I had in my hand was a little revolver, an idea I didn't even know I had about myself until she kissed me, still as a doll in my arms, telling me about the stories that go bad inside you. Inside me. And she was sorry about the life I didn't know I had that wasn't worth having anyway.

I'm looking but not seeing the edge of an envelope slipping out from behind the landscape, the photo in it of an old man falling out of an office window and a woman with her hand just drawing away from the old man's shoulder, her hair stringy blonde, dry as straw, like someone in drag. Behind me, on its side, a crystal decanter leaking brandy onto the lacquered end table, around a cut-glass ashtray, as if someone tried to get a drink and left in a hurry,

7

the Author home from his dingy business, taking a shower, brushing back his wet hair, picking out bits of wig, feeling good for the first time in weeks. His wife strong enough to sit with him at dinner the

way she used to. Some candles. Some bubbly. A smile. Chopin play-
ing on the Victrola.

God happy in His heaven.

After Raymond Chandler's novel *The High Window* (1942)
and the life of Raymond Chandler (1888–1959)

THE RIDE HOME

THE RIDE HOME

Greyhound from L.A. to Frisco, the steep fall from the coastal high-way toward the sea like Joan Crawford in a convertible out of control, my lost job tumbling down the slope. Whatever's been chasing me not finding me. Not my landlady's husband in Culver City, her body's rent coming due again, not him roaring out of the driveway, tracking the absence that was really himself. Savings account cleaned out, my file empty, the man who wasn't here, my mind always crossing a river, to visit a sick father. Mother looking thin and forgotten. A sister who keeps moving back in. Now it's Nob Hill, the boardinghouse, the girl at breakfast telling me I've a funny accent. Another long street leading down to water. Something changing. Something drowned. The cottage back in Culver City coated with the dust from a B-movie set, the blow her husband landed on my head a geography I stumble through.

Imagine being in the mountains, looking at the stars, remembering. Imagine a city with trees blooming in tenements. A background music so low that Sol the grocer leaves his store to listen. Imagine no down payment. A world of credit, where sister survives. Poetry in the streets, cafés, the asylum. Prophecy streaking my mind on a regular basis. Imagine being inside the film, looking out. Father in the Studio Bar on 34th Avenue, lighting a cigarette in the glow of the Schaeffer's sign. Mother not, after all these years, getting groceries on the cuff. Imagine me riding to rescue no one. Not even myself. The credits rolling down the sky, along the road, name after name.

North now. Fog. The bus blocked by snow in the Sierra Nevada pass. I stumble out to get some air, in a khaki trench coat. Pee into a blinding whiteness. Back on board, the soldiers going to Chicago think I'm an officer, my speech bright with souvenirs. Later, down from the mountain, we stop in a town like a border town. There's the government man from *Ride the Pink Horse* eating in the Café of Three Violets, stabbing toast into the yolks of eggs, a yellowish stain on the tips of his fingers like sulfa used to treat a wound. Children wearing amulets from the Mexican provinces, dresses stitched by their mothers, they think the man in the trench coat is checking visas. The girl wearing her grandmother's shawl, the girl who sees me with nowhere in my eyes, says, "I saw you dead last night." I laugh and her darkness opens into smiles.

She will tell her story from town to town. The officer who waved from the bus. She will make me huge as an army trampling through corn.

DEMOLITION

Gone, the Mayan Revival exterior; torn down, the darkness;
     rubble shaped into homes with
common walls; first-floor stores dreaming behind their windows
of pleated skirts, high heels, a silvery music. Take away the stairs,
     the velvety hangings, the *zing* of small-caliber

bullets, phony blackmail letters, yesterday's clues. The sugar
     dots of nonpareils I can still taste on my tongue
are an abacus for the number of steps I'd taken across that floor.
Dissolving tiles in a mosaic, bits of a scene I couldn't recognize
     until I was halfway to the balcony

and looked through the dust-scented air at the blanks of missing
     tapestries. I'm up there, on a floating height,
gazing down on myself, on the ruins of the candy stand,
on the spirits of thousands risen from their own forgetfulness—
     a vast emptiness

where they wait for someone to restore a dark colloquy.
     The names of Illinois,
Nebraska, Colorado, Utah, Nevada, California, the peeled
labels from a suitcase. As if I'd come home with a vocabulary
     half my own. Half ghost.

AUTHOR'S NOTE

During the time I worked on this collection, 1998–2002, many people have helped. Dan Masterson very early on saw how these poems might go and kept me at the work. Floyd Skloot encouraged me after seeing a crude, early draft. Jay Meek cheered me on significantly, and not only by taking poems for *North Dakota Quarterly*. My brother Dan has been enthusiastic about these poems and made it possible to view dozens of *noir* films thanks to his video tapes. David Mairowitz all the way from Avignon helped me celebrate the energy of *noir*. Nancy Hazelton and Reamy Jansen have been avid readers of these poems as I completed them. Thanks to Barbara Epler, Peggy Fox, and Griselda Ohannessian at New Directions for their good advice on the first version of this book. Peter Glassgold, friend and editor of my doings with New Directions for such a long time, showed me how to make a final version even better. He also gave invaluable advice on *Inhabited World: New & Selected Poems 1970–1995*. Eileen, what can I say? For more than forty years, you've been there, saying what it is and what it isn't. Telling the truth and with love.

—J.A.